Animal Babies

Piglets

by Meg Gaertner

FOCUS READERS

SCOUT

www.focusreaders.com

Focus Readers is distributed by North Star Editions:
sales@northstareditions.com | 888-417-0195

Produced for Focus Readers by Red Line Editorial.

Photographs ©: mikedabell/iStockphoto, cover, 1; tratong/Shutterstock Images, 4, 16 (top left); James Copeland/iStockphoto, 7; LAByrne/iStockphoto, 9; Budimir Jevtic/Shutterstock Images, 11 (top); Erika J Mitchell/Shutterstock Images, 11 (bottom), 16 (top right); Erkki Makkonen/Shutterstock Images, 13 (top), 16 (bottom left); redmal/iStockphoto, 13 (bottom), 16 (bottom right); Slavko Sereda/Shutterstock Images, 15

Library of Congress Cataloging-in-Publication Data
Names: Gaertner, Meg, author.
Title: Piglets / by Meg Gaertner.
Description: Lake Elmo, MN : Focus Readers, [2020] | Series: Animal babies | Audience: K to Grade 3. | Includes index. |
Identifiers: LCCN 2018060033 (print) | LCCN 2018061646 (ebook) | ISBN 9781641859561 (PDF) | ISBN 9781641858878 (ebook) | ISBN 9781641857499 (hardcover) | ISBN 9781641858182 (paperback)
Subjects: LCSH: Piglets--Juvenile literature.
Classification: LCC SF395.5 (ebook) | LCC SF395.5 .G34 2020 (print) | DDC 636.4/07--dc23
LC record available at https://lccn.loc.gov/2018060033

Printed in the United States of America
Mankato, MN
May, 2019

About the Author

Meg Gaertner is a children's book editor and author. She lives in Minneapolis, Minnesota. When not writing, she is usually dancing or spending time outside.

Table of Contents

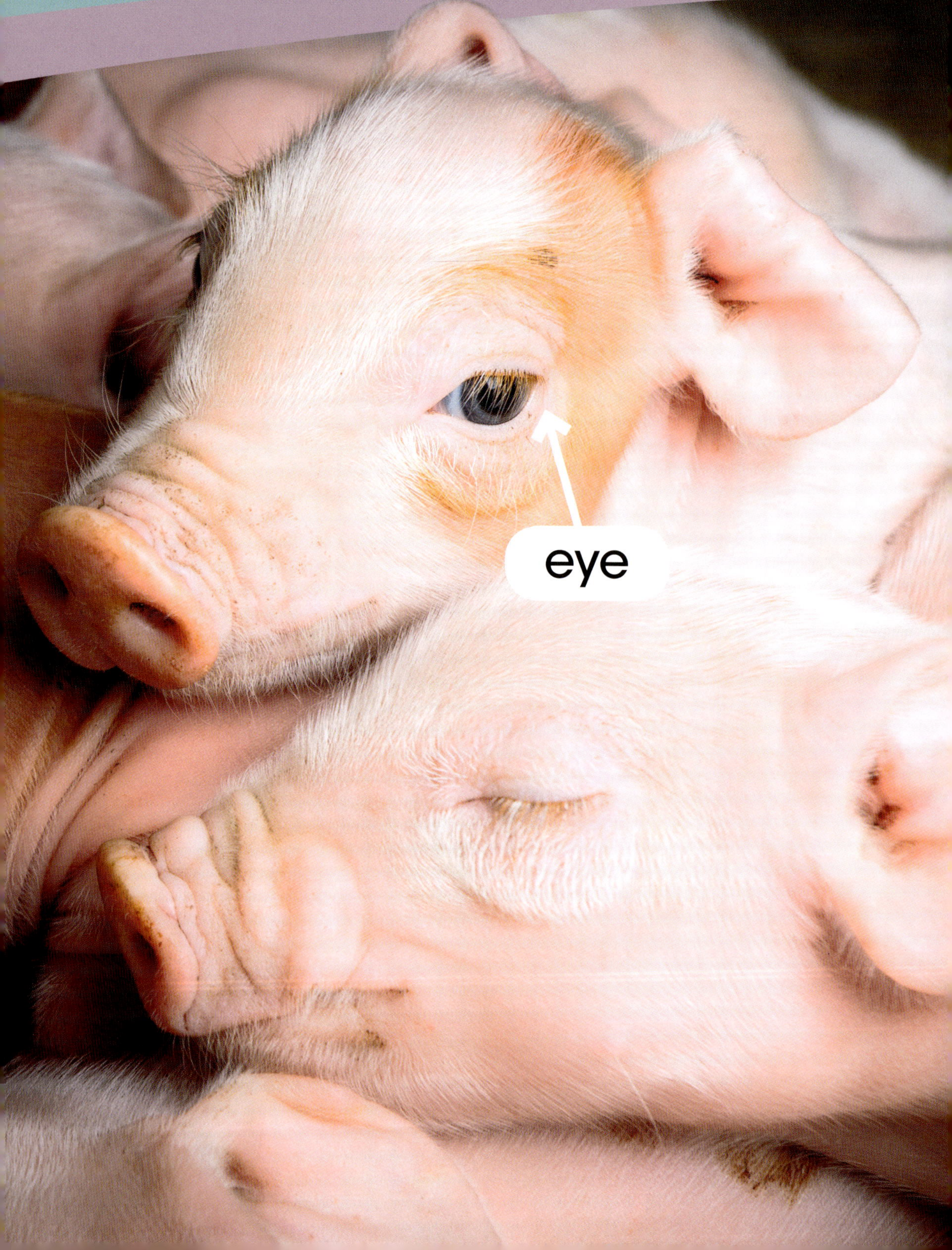
eye

First Days

Piglets are baby pigs.
A mother has
many piglets.
They open their **eyes**.

Piglets stand up.

They stay with their mother.

They drink her milk.

Piglets stay close together. They keep one another warm.

Changes

Piglets grow up.

They walk around.

They have strong **noses**.

They smell for food.

nose

Piglets dig for food.

They eat **leaves**.

They eat **roots**.

leaves

roots

Growing Up

Piglets keep growing.

They get bigger.

They live in groups.

Glossary

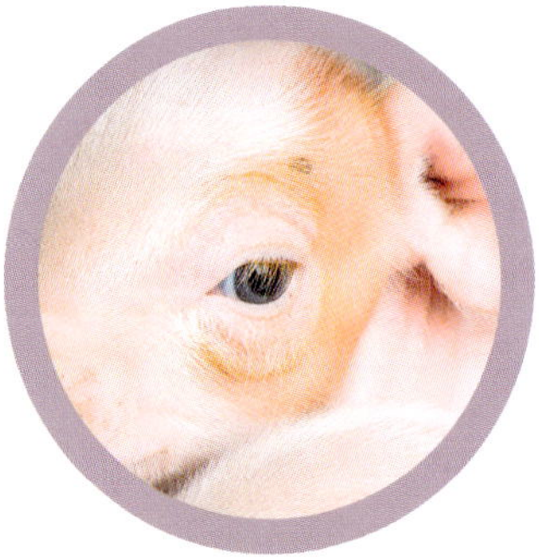

eyes

noses

leaves

roots

Index